Welsh

It's Wales

Organic
Recipes

Salads, Soups and Sauces from Wales

Dave Frost
recipes by Barbara Rottner Frost

y Lolfa

By the same authors:

Welsh Salad Days

Food and drink from Wales to the end of the world

086243 383 5

£8.95

First impression: 2001

© Copyright Dave Frost and Y Lolfa Cyf., 2001

Cover design: Ceri Jones

ISBN: 0 86243 574 9

Printed on acid free and partly recycled paper
and published and bound in Wales by:
Y Lolfa Cyf., Talybont, Ceredigion SY24 5AP
e-mail ylolfa@ylolfa.com
internet www.ylolfa.com
phone +44 (0)1970 832 304
fax 832 782
isdn 832 813

Contents

Introduction

These are recipes we use at home. Many of the salads and dressings were first prepared by my wife, Barbara, when we ran an organic salad shop in Aberystwyth. To complete our recipes from Wales we have also included soups and sauces. Some of these are new; the others are versions of classic recipes.

Wales has been in the forefront of many developments in organic farming, and the National Assembly is now setting the pace with targets for organic agriculture, grants to assist farmers and growers who are converting and funding for the Organic Centre of Excellence in Aberystwyth.

There are many reasons for the great surge in popularity of organic farming. It's seen as a more environmentally-friendly way of growing crops, it has a genuine concern for animal welfare, and, above all, it produces high quality food without using GMOs, additives or pesticides. The link between diet and health lies at the core of organic farming and growing: a healthy soil produces healthy crops, which are the basis of a healthy diet.

We eat salads throughout the year, daily, with every main meal – but it's not a penance. These are meals made with in-season organically grown ingredients, spiced with herbs and fruit and served with homemade dressings. It's all food to enjoy.

Apparently fewer and fewer people are cooking meals at home, and those who do tend increasingly to eat more processed and convenience food and less fresh vegetables. Nutritionists and health officials tells us that this is bad for our health and the current advice recommends more fresh fruit and vegetables more foods rich in dietary fibre, less fat, less salt and less sugary food. Above all, for health reasons we are urged to eat fresh rather than preserved, packaged or convenience foods and to eat plenty of fresh vegetables because raw or lightly cooked food retains the highest nutritional value.

This all makes very good sense, but it's also good advice because eating fresh food, raw and lightly cooked organic vegetables is delicious – especially when they are served with an appetising sauce or salad dressing.

One reason given for the increase in convenience food is the pace of life. Few people it seems now have time to prepare and cook food at home. Many children and young people, or so we are told, grow up without having seen their parents cook a meal, but the popularity of cookery books and programmes is evidence that many want to learn. All is not lost, and help is at hand. Salads are among the easiest and quickest meals to prepare and using crisp, fresh organic vegetables and herbs, with their pungent aromas and instant tastes are a stimulating introduction to the whole enjoyment of food and cooking. Enjoy !

Dave Frost

February 2001

Salads

Mixed leaf salad

Use any mixture of leaf salads available according to season. Preferably choose different colours and textures. A short soaking of lettuce in warm water will remove unwanted bitterness. For example:

1 little gem lettuce

½ iceberg lettuce

1 small lolla rosso or some leaves of a red oak leaf salad bowl

1 Frise endive or Batavian lettuce

bunch of mixed herbs e.g. parsley, mint, lemon balm, marjoram, fennel edible flowers e.g. marigold, borage, and/or nasturtium petals

vinaigrette dressing

Coarsely chop lettuce or endive with a sharp knife (a blunt knife will bruise the leaves) and soak them in luke warm water. Drain and dry well. Add chopped fresh herbs and toss the mixture in a vinaigrette dressing just prior to serving. Garnish the salad with edible flowers.

Mushroom salad with chives

¾ lb/350 g button mushrooms

bunch of chives, spring onions or a small red onion

mayonnaise dressing

sage flowers

Choose mushrooms that are fresh, firm and small. Wash them thoroughly. Bring a saucepan of salted water to the boil and tip the mushrooms into the water. Cover the saucepan with a lid. Leave them to blanch for five minutes then strain through a colander and leave to cool.

Chop some chives very finely. Tip the cooled mushrooms into a bowl, cover with mayonnaise, add the chives and stir well. The bowl can be decorated with sage flowers. When chives are not available, spring onions or red skinned salad onions can be substituted. For garlic mushrooms, use garlic mayonnaise for the dressing.

Mixed beansprouts with rocket and spring onions

6 oz/175 g beansprouts/alfalfa

bunch of rocket leaves

bunch of spring onions

lemon and oil dressing

Fill a bowl with lukewarm water. Empty the beansprouts and/or alfalfa into the bowl and wash them well. Skim off the husks with a small sieve or a tea strainer. Tip the cleaned beansprouts into a colander and drain them well. Clean the rocket and spring onions, chop them finely and mix well with the beansprouts.

For a dressing, use olive oil, lemon juice, black pepper and salt or a lemon juice mayonnaise. If rocket is not available, finely chopped radicchio or raw sliced button mushrooms can be used as substitutes.

Alfalfa, mushroom and radish

½ lb/225 g alfalfa

½ lb/225 g mushrooms

bunch of radish

Finely slice the radishes and prepare the salad as for mixed beansprouts. For the dressing, use a blend of sunflower oil, lemon juice, salt and black pepper.

Grated carrot salad

6 new season carrots

bunch of chervil, mint or parsley

mayonnaise or yogurt dressing

Wash six young carrots and grate them finely. Chop some chervil (or mint or parsley). Mix the grated carrot and the herbs together thoroughly and serve with a mayonnaise or yogurt dressing.

Cooked carrot salad

6 medium sized carrots

sprig of lovage

salt

oil and vinegar dressing

sesame seeds

Wash and dice six medium carrots. Add a sprig of lovage to a pan of salted water and cook the carrots for about five minutes until tender. Drain the carrots and allow to cool; remove the lovage and add an oil and vinegar dressing. Sprinkle the salad with sesame seeds.

Beetroot salad

Bunch of new season beetroots, or twelve small ones. (Small baby beetroots, no more than the size of a tomato are the most delicious.)

I red skinned salad onion or 2/3 shallots

oil and vinegar dressing

Boil the beetroot in salt water until tender, then drain them and allow to cool. Peel off the skins of the beetroot and slice them finely, but if they are very small they can just be quartered. Use red skinned salad onions, thinly sliced to add to the beetroot.

Make a dressing of oil, vinegar (elderflower vinegar is best), sugar and salt. Pour the dressing over the beetroot and allow to marinate for 2 to 3 hours, or as long as possible.

Welsh onions, spring onions or shallots can be used as a substitute for the red onions.

In the spring, home grown and freshly harvested beetroot leaves can also be used to make a salad. Wash the tender young leaves, then steam them briefly. Cool and garnish with finely chopped chives.

Courgettes and cherry tomatoes

Use green or yellow varieties of courgettes; the yellow varieties, like Goldrush, tend to be sweeter. Choose small, finger sized courgettes wherever possible.

1 medium sliced courgette

½lb/225g cherry tomatoes

bunch of basil (purple basil if available)

vinaigrette dressing

Slice one medium sized courgette thinly and halve a pound (450 g) of cherry tomatoes. Chop green or purple basil finely and mix the ingredients well. Toss the salad in a light vinaigrette dressing.

Tomatoes with little gem lettuce and marjoram

2 little gem lettuce or 1 cos lettuce

½lb/225 g tomatoes

bunch marjoram

oil and vinegar dressing

Chop two little gem lettuce and soak in warm water.

Slice half a pound (225 g) of tomatoes. Chop the fresh marjoram and mix the ingredients together well. Toss the salad in a dressing made from vinegar, oil, salt and sugar. A variation on this salad is to use pak choi instead of little gem.

Fennel and tomato salad

½lb/225 g tomatoes

2 medium bulbs florence fennel

juice of I lemon

I tablespoon olive oil

salt

black pepper

Quarter the tomatoes and let them drain. Halve two medium sized fennel bulbs and cut off and save the green tops for a garnish. Slice the fennel as you would an onion to make rings. Toss the fennel in lemon juice to prevent it browning. Mix together with the tomato and toss in a little olive oil, salt and black pepper.

Cooked fennel salad

½lb/225 g tomatoes

2 medium bulbs of Florence fennel

salt

black pepper

tablespoon olive oil or sunflower oil

Plunge the tomatoes into boiling water for several minutes; this makes them easy to peel. Peel and slice the tomatoes. Slice two medium sized fennel bulbs lengthways (the opposite direction to making rings) and fry briefly on both sides in oil; add a pinch of salt and some black pepper. Leave the fennel to cool, then layer them together with the sliced and peeled tomatoes. Serve the dish when fully cold and garnish with the fronds from the fennel tops, some olive oil and lemon juice.

Cucumber with dill and borage flowers

Use ridge cucumbers if they are available; mini cucumbers are also very good.

1 cucumber or 2 mini cucumbers

1 red salad onion or bunch of spring onions

bunch of dill

borage flowers

oil and vinegar dressing

salt

black pepper

teaspoon brown sugan

Slice one cucumber or two mini cucumbers finely and put them in a colander to drain. Slice one red salad onion finely, or finely chop a bunch of spring onions. Chop the fresh dill. Mix a dressing of oil, vinegar, salt and sugar. Mix the cucumber and onions together and pour the dressing over the mixture. Garnish with freshly picked borage flowers.

Crisp lettuce and melon

Home grown melons are likely to be the small sweet Cantaloupe variety, but shop bought Honeydew, Ogen or Galia melons will do fine. Mint or lemon balm complements the sweetness of the melon perfectly.

1 crisp lettuce

bunch of mint or lemon balm

1 melon

yogurt or lemon mayonnaise dressing

Chop a crisp lettuce finely and soak in warm water, then drain well. Chop the mint or lemon balm. Quarter the melon and spoon out the seeds. Peel the quarters and dice the melon into ½ inch or 1.5 cm cubes. Mix the ingredients together well and use a yogurt or lemon mayonnaise dressing.

Red lettuce with cucumbers and onion rings

This salad is best with 'oak leaf' or 'lollo rosso' lettuce, red onions and ridge cucumbers.

1 red lettuce

1 cucumber or 2 mini cucumbers

1 onion

oil and vinegar dressing

teaspoon sugar

Chop the lettuce and soak in warm water, then drain. Slice the cucumber finely and drain. Cut a whole onion into rings, slicing it very finely. Mix the ingredients together and toss well in a dressing of elderflower vinegar, oil, sugar and salt.

For a variation on this salad, simply mix the chopped red lettuce with edible flowers: nasturtium, marigold, sweet rocket, borage and heartsease, then toss in the dressing.

Mixed sweet pepper salad

1 small yellow pepper

1 small red pepper

1 small green pepper

bunch of spring onions or a red salad onion

oil and lemon dressing

Choose one each of small yellow, red and green peppers. Cut the peppers into thin strips after removing the stalk and the seeds. Mix the pepper strips with chopped spring onions or a sliced red onion. Dress with oil, vinegar, salt and sugar.

For a variation on this salad, prepare the peppers as above and mix with chopped lettuce. Use a crisp lettuce like Webbs Wonderful, Little Gem hearts or a Batavian lettuce. Chop the lettuce finely, soak in warm water for three minutes, then drain well. Dress as above. For a further variation, substitute celery for the lettuce.

Green bean salad with onions

This recipe is for cooked French dwarf beans, but all kinds of fresh green beans can be used, including young broad beans.

½lb/225 g French beans or ½lb/225 g shelled broad beans

desert spoon of salt

bunch summer savoury

I red salad onion

oil and vinegar dressing

Top and tail the beans and chop into ½ inch/I cm pieces; or for broad beans, shell from the pods. Bring a pan of water to the boil and add double the normal quantity of salt. Put the beans in the boiling water together with a good sprig of winter savoury, then cook until the beans are tender; this should only take 2 to 3 minutes. To keep the beans a good green colour drain them quickly, then steep them in ice cold water until completely cold. Drain them well. Mix oil, elderflower vinegar, sugar and salt and pour over the beans. Leave to marinate for two or three hours if possible. Chop a red onion finely and sprinkle with black pepper and mix into the salad.

This salad can be made into a more substantial meal by adding ½ lb/225g peeled and quartered tomatoes or halved cherry tomatoes.

N.B. Let the prepared tomatoes drain well before adding them to the beans, otherwise they can make the salad too watery.

Celeriac salad with land cress or lamb's lettuce

1 medium or 1 large celeriac

teaspoon of lemon juice or vinegar

1 red salad onion

salt

bunch of land cress, Lamb's lettuce or salad cress

oil and vinegar dressing

Peel the celeriac and cut into slices. Boil in salted water with a teaspoon of lemon juice or vinegar to preserve the white colour of the celeriac. Cook until tender, about 5 to 10 minutes. Drain and leave to cool. Chop a red onion into very fine rings. Carefully wash and clean the land cress or Lamb's lettuce; if using the latter, pay particular attention to the base of the leaves where the matted roots tend to hold the soil. Mix the ingredients together and dress with a mixture of oil, elderflower vinegar and salt.

Leek, apple and walnut salad

1 medium or 4 small leeks

2 apples (crisp red skinned apples are best)

2 tablespoons walnuts

vinaigrette dressing

Chop the leeks very finely, then soak in lukewarm water and drain well.
Quarter and core two apples and slice thinly. Crisp red skinned apples are
best. Soak them in lemon juice to stop them browning. Chop a handful of
walnuts into small pieces. Mix all the ingredients together. Toss the salad in
a vinaigrette dressing just prior to serving.

Chinese cabbage with 'Mizuna' and orange

½ chinese cabbage

bunch 'Mizuna'

1 orange, small bunch of grapes or 1 pink grapefruit

Chop half a Chinese cabbage and a bunch of 'Mizuna' finely; soak in lukewarm water, then drain well. Peel and quarter an orange, then slice the quarters finely. Drain, then mix the ingredients together. Toss the salad in a yogurt or lemon and oil dressing.

For variations on this salad, grapes or grapefruit can be used instead of the orange. The grapes should be washed and halved before using. Grapefruits, especially the pink fleshed Ruby Red grapefruit, are an excellent substitute for either orange or grapes. They need to be peeled, quartered and then sliced thinly before mixing with the other ingredients.

Endive, radiccio and pineapple

Either 'Frisée' endive or the broad leaved variety can be used in this salad.

1 endive

1 radicchio

1 small pineapple or 1 orange

yogurt or lemon and oil dressing

Chop the endive finely, cut the radicchio in half and slice very finely into long thin strips. Soak both in warm water. Drain well. Peel and core the pineapple (i.e. cut out the stem). Chop into small cubes and mix with the endive and radiccio. Toss in a yogurt or lemon and oil dressing. Sliced orange can be used as a substitute for the pineapple.

Celery, carrot and pepper salad

1 stick celery

1 green pepper

2 medium carrots

1 oz/25 g celery leaves or a bunch of parsley

(preferably broad leafed parsley)

yogurt or vinaigrette dressing

Chop the celery finely, soak in warm water for three minutes, then drain well. Halve and clean the pepper, removing all of the seeds and cut into fine long strips. Peel the carrot and cut into thin slices; rinse them well. Add one ounce of finely chopped wild celery leaves or parsley (preferably broad leaved parsley). Mix the ingredients together well and toss in yogurt dressing or vinaigrette.

Cabbage salad and 'Mizuna'

1 hard white cabbage

bunch 'Mizuna' or parsley

chive flowers or marigold petals

mayonnaise or lemon mayonnaise dressing

Quarter the cabbage and grate it finely. Chop the mizuna finely. Mix well and dress with mayonnaise or lemon mayonnaise. If available, decorate the salad with chive flowers or marigold petals. Parsley makes an excellent substitute for the 'Mizuna'.

Cabbage salad with hot dressing

1 hard white cabbage

bunch parsley

¼ lb/125 g streaky bacon

oil and vinegar dressing

salt

black pepper

Proceed as above but use parsley, not 'Mizuna'. Chop streaky bacon into small cubes and fry until completely crisp. While still hot, pour the bacon and the hot fat over the cabbage and mix well. Add a small amount of the following dressing: oil, vinegar, sugar, salt and ground black pepper.

Red cabbage salad with pear

Red cabbage stores very well, and like hard white cabbage it is available throughout the winter.

1 red cabbage

1 firm pear

juice of 1 lemon

tablespoon walnuts

yogurt dressing

Quarter the red cabbage and remove the inner stalk. Grate the cabbage finely. Quarter and slice a pear and soak in lemon juice to prevent it browning in the salad. Mix the pear and cabbage together and serve with a yogurt dressing. Chopped walnuts can be added to this salad.

Chicory and orange salad

3 good sized heads of chicory

I orange

bunch parsley, watercress, rocket or lamb's lettuce

lemon and oil dressing

Halve the chicory and remove the base which tends to be very bitter. Slice the chicory finely and put in lukewarm water for three minutes. Drain well. While the chicory is draining peel, slice and cube an orange. To add some colour, roughly chop one of the following: parsley, watercress, rocket or lamb's lettuce; or, if available, sprouted sunflower seeds. Put the chicory, orange and green garnish together in a bowl and mix well. Make a dressing of lemon juice, sunflower oil, salt and black pepper. Add the dressing to the salad just before serving to preserve the crispness of the chicory.

Calabrese, cauliflower and clementines

I small cauliflower or ½ large cauliflower

2 clementines or I orange

½lb/225 g or 2 heads of calabrese

vinaigrette or yogurt dressing

Wash and chop the cauliflower and calabrese into florets. Peel two clementines or one orange and divide into segments. Mix the ingredients together well and dress with a vinaigrette or yogurt dressing.

Cooked cauliflower salad

I small cauliflower or ½ large cauliflower

bunch parsley

black pepper

salt

yogurt dressing

Wash and chop one small cauliflower. Cook in salted water until tender, about five to ten minutes. Drain the cauliflower and cool. Toss in a yogurt dressing with freshly ground black pepper and finely chopped parsley.

Fruit Salad

Melon, banana and orange are the all year round basis of fruit salad to which fresh fruit of each season can be added. In summer peach, blackcurrants, strawberry and raspberry are added, In autumn blackberries, plums and grapes are in season.

The fruit should be washed, peeled and chopped as required, then strained through a colander. Banana, apple and pears should be soaked in lemon juice to preserve their colour. Sugar can be added according to taste and sunflower seeds add an extra dimension. Cream or Greek style yogurt finishes off the fruit salad.

Potato salad

3 lbs/1½kg potatoes

chives or parsley

vinaigrette dressing

Wash the potatoes but do not peel them. Depending on their size, halve or quarter the potatoes and boil them in salted water, then drain. Leave them until cool enough to handle. Peel the still warm potatoes (they peel easiest when still warm) then set aside to cool completely before slicing.

Slice the potatoes thinly and add finely chopped chives or parsley to taste. Add a generous amount of vinaigrette dressing and leave to soak for two hours, or if possible overnight.

Potato salad with hot dressing

3 lbs/1½ potatoes

chives or parsley

3 rashers streaky bacon

for the dressing:

1 tablespoon wine vinegar

5 tablespoons oil

sugar, salt and black pepper

Cook and slice the potatoes as above and mix with the parsley or chives. Chop three rashers of streaky bacon into small cubes and fry until completely crisp. While still hot, pour the cubes of bacon and the fat over the potatoes and mix in well. Add a small amount of oil and vinegar mixed with salt and sugar. Add ground black pepper.

Asparagus salad

bunch of asparagus (about 1 lb/450 g)

salt

white wine vinegar, salt, sugar and sunflower oil (for a salad dressing)

Peel the lower stems of the asparagus and place them upright in a pan of warm water so they are nearly submerged. Add salt and cook until tender (this will depend on the thickness of the stems). Drain the asparagus and reserve the water to make soup and/or a salad dressing. Either serve the asparagus hot with a simple sauce of melted butter, or cold as a salad.

For the salad, make a dressing using some of the reserved water from cooking, with the vinegar and a pinch of salt.

Globe artichoke vinaigrette

1 globe artichoke per person

salt

vinaigrette dressing

Cook the whole artichokes in salted water until the stems are tender. This will take between 15 and 20 minutes depending on size. Drain and allow to cool. Serve the artichokes with bowls of vinaigrette to dip leaves into.

Soups

Asparagus soup

water preserved from cooking asparagus (see asparagus salad recipe)

2 oz/50 g butter

1 oz/25 g flour

small pot of cream

salt and pepper (preferably cayenne pepper)

glass of white wine

juice of 1 lemon

Mix the flour with half of the butter, then combine the mixture with the asparagus water. Add the cream, then strain the soup through a fine sieve. Mix in the white wine and the lemon juice. Season with salt and pepper to taste. Heat the soup and, just before serving, mix in the rest of the cold butter.

Celeriac Soup

1 medium onion

½ medium sized celeriac

2 tablespoons sunflower oil or 2oz/50g margarine

1 tablespoon vinegar or juice of 1 lemon

salt

teaspoon brown sugar

pinch of nutmeg

½ pint/150 ml of milk

¼ pint/75 ml of cream

1 glass medium dry white wine

for the garnish:

sprig parsley and black pepper or fried breadcrumbs

Finely chop the onion and fry till golden in the oil or margarine. Chop the celeriac into small cubes and add to the onion. Fry together briefly. Cover the vegetables with water and bring to the boil. Add salt to taste, and mix in the vinegar or lemon and the nutmeg. Simmer for about 10 minutes until the ingredients are soft. Take off the heat then blend the mixture in a liquidiser until smooth. Add the milk, wine and cream and re-heat without boiling. Serve in bowls garnished with the finely chopped parsley and black pepper or the fried breadcrumbs.

Mushroom soup

1 onion

½lb/225 g mushrooms (field mushrooms or brown chestnut mushrooms

have the best flavour)

2 oz/50 g butter or margarine

soy sauce

salt and pepper

½pint/150 ml milk

2 oz/50 g cream

glass white wine

for the garnish:

bunch chives

Chop the onion finely and fry in the butter or margarine till soft. Slice the mushrooms and add to the onion. Sprinkle with soy sauce. Fry together until the mushrooms are cooked through. Add some milk and simmer gently. Add salt and pepper to taste. Blend in a liquidiser until smooth. Return to the saucepan adding the cream and white wine to taste. Heat through then serve sprinkled with finely chopped chives.

Herb soup

I small onion, finely chopped

2 small potatoes, chopped small

2 oz/50 g chervil

I oz/25 g parsley

sprig of lemon balm or small bunch of chives

juice of I lemon

2 cups water, I glass white wine

½ teaspoon brown sugar

2 oz/50 g butter

salt and pepper

small pot of cream

Fry the onions and the potatoes, then add two-thirds of the finely chopped herbs and the water. Add salt, pepper, lemon juice and brown sugar to taste. Bring the mixture to the boil and simmer gently for a few minutes. During cooking, the potatoes thicken the soup, and they are used in preference to flour for this purpose. Liquidise then strain. Season with white wine and cream. As the herbs tend to go grey when cooked in the soup, keep back a third of the chopped herbs and combine them with 2 oz/50 g of butter to make a herb butter. Just before serving, add the dark green herb butter and whisk it well. This both gives the herb soup a better colour and helps to thicken it.

Chervil Soup

2 shallots or small onions

2 medium sized potatoes

1 oz/25 g butter for frying

1 oz/25 g softened butter

glass of white wine

small tot of Pernod (or any other pastis)

large bunch of fresh chervil, finely chopped

2 pints stock (preferably beef stock)

small pot of cream

salt and pepper

Peel and slice the potatoes and onions. Cook them in butter until the onions become transparent. Add the wine and the Pernod, most of the chopped chervil (but save some to add at the end) and the stock. Bring to the boil and simmer gently until the potatoes are soft. Strain the mixture through a sieve, purée the solids, then return them to the liquid. Add the cream and season to taste. While the soup is re-heating, mix the softened butter with the remaining chervil and fold this into the soup prior to serving. The chervil butter enhances the fresh chervil taste and gives the soup a good bright green colour.

Sorrel soup

½lb/225 g sorrel

2 small potatoes, chopped very small

1 small onion

¼ pint/75ml milk

glass of white wine

salt, sugar, pepper

pot of plain yogurt

parsley or chives

Chop the onion finely and fry until transparent. Mix in the potatoes and add two-thirds of the well washed and roughly chopped sorrel. Fry briefly, then cover the sorrel with water. Simmer for 5 minutes and add salt, pepper and sugar to taste. The potatoes will break up and thicken the soup and they are used in preference to flour for this purpose. Add the milk, then liquidise the soup and add the wine. The remaining sorrel leaves should be finely chopped and mixed with the butter and formed into small balls. Just before serving, stir in the sorrel butter balls to give the soup an extra green colour and to give it extra creaminess. Top the soup with the yogurt, which is an excellent substitute for soured cream, and serve sprinkled with finely chopped parsley or chives.

Leek and potato soup

1 medium onion

3 meium leeks

4 medium potatoes

2 tablespoons sunflower oil or 2 oz/50 g margarine

desert spoon of caraway

salt and pepper

2 oz/50 g cream

optional:

1 teaspoon mild curry powder

glass of white wine

2 rashers bacon

Melt the margarine or oil and add the curry powder, finely chopped onion and/or the bacon. Fry until golden brown. Add the peeled and sliced potatoes and mix in with the onion and bacon plus the caraway. Cover with water and add salt to taste. Bring to the boil then add the washed and chopped leeks, then cook until the potatoes and leeks are soft. Liquidise ¾s of the soup until it is smooth. Mix the liquidised portion with the remainder of the soup and add cream and wine to taste. Re-heat the soup without boiling then sprinkle with black pepper and serve.

Sauces and Dressings

Sweet and savoury mayonnaise

2 eggs

1½ pint/275 ml sunflower oil

½ teaspoon salt

½ tablespoon sugar

1½ tablespoons wholegrain honey mustard

1 tablespoon white wine vinegar

1 pot low fat yogurt

Break the eggs into a blender and whisk until foaming and nearly white. Slowly pour in the oil with the blender still whisking. Add the vinegar, using only a small quantity for flavouring. Now add the salt, sugar and mustard. Whisk it all together in the blender and thin to the desired consistency with the yogurt. If kept covered, or in a screw-topped jar, the mayonnaise will keep for several days in a refrigerator.

Garlic mayonnaise

2 eggs

½ pint/275 ml sunflower oil or cold-pressed grape seed oil

2 tablespoons mild mustard

½ tablespoon salt

juice of two lemons

3 large cloves garlic

1 pot low fat yogurt

Put the eggs in a blender and whisk until foaming and nearly white. Slowly add in the oil. Add the mustard, salt and the lemon juice. Crush the garlic cloves, add them to the mixture and whisk it all together in the blender. Thin with the yogurt.

Lemon mayonnaise

2 eggs

½ pint/275 ml sunflower oil or cold-pressed grape seed oil

1 tablespoon mild mustard

1 tablespoon salt

juice of two lemons

1 pot low fat yogurt

Whiz the eggs in a blender until foaming and nearly white. Slowly add the oil with the blender still whisking. Add the mustard, salt and lemon juice and whisk them all together. Thin to the desired consistency with the yogurt.

Tofu vegetarian mayonnaise

1 pack or ¼ lb/110 g tofu

¼ pint/150 ml olive oil

¼ pint/150 ml white wine vinegar

¼ teaspoon dill

1 teaspoon honey

Whiz the tofu in a blender. Add the oil slowly, then the seasoning, vinegar and honey. Adjust the honey and seasoning to taste. Caraway seed can be used instead of dill if the mayonnaise is to be used to bind coleslaw, and tarragon can be substituted when the mayonnaise is used to dress cold cooked vegetables.

Tahini dressing

1 tablespoon plain yogurt

2 tablespoons light tahini

juice of one lemon

garlic salt and black pepper

chopped chives

lovage

Combine the garlic salt and black pepper with the lemon juice, then blend in the yogurt and the tahini. This is a good substitute for mayonnaise with new potatoes. Sprinkle with chopped chives and lovage.

Vinaigrette dressing

½ pint/275 ml stock

1 ½ tablespoons mustard

2 tablespoons brown sugar

¼ pint/150 ml white wine vinegar

1 teaspoon salt

3/4 pint/425 ml sunflower oil

Mix the mustard and sunflower oil and blend well to a mayonnaise-like consistency. Blend in the brown sugar, and salt to taste. To this mixture add the vinegar. At this point it should be strong tasting as the stock is mixed in at the end to thin the vinaigrette down. Add the stock and stir well. This is a basic vinaigrette dressing and we modify it, using different herb or fruit vinegars, depending on the particular salad to be dressed. The vinaigrette will keep for several weeks in an airtight container in a cool place. Always stir it well before using.

Yogurt dressing

I tablespoon stock

I pot low fat yogurt

salt

chopped parsley, chervil, chive or mint

Stir the stock into the yogurt. Add salt to taste and add the chopped herb for flavour and decoration.

Lemon and oil dressing

juice of two lemons

½ pint/275 ml sunflower oil or cold-pressed grape seed oil or olive oil

I tablespoon salt

freshly ground black pepper

Mix the lemon juice and the oil together with the salt and the pepper. Add the dressing to the salad just before serving to preserve the crispness. For some particularly strongly flavoured salads, such as those with rocket and spring onions, olive oil can be used in preference to the milder sunflower or grape seed oils.

Mushroom Sauce

½ lb/225 g button mushrooms

I small onion

¼ lb/110 g butter or margarine

½ pint/150 ml of cream

I desert spoon of soy sauce

salt and cayenne pepper

Peel and chop the onion very finely. Wash the mushrooms and cut into quarters. Melt the butter or margarine in a good sized frying pan and when hot add the chopped onion. Swet the onion in the fat, but do not let them burn or go brown. When the onions are soft and translucent add the mushrooms and a sprinkle of salt. Turn down the heat and let the mushrooms cook through (about 8 minutes). When the mushrooms are cooked add the cream, then stir in the soy sauce. Allow to simmer for several minutes but do not let the mixture boil. Add salt and pepper to taste and serve immediately. Excellent with pasta, boiled or mashed potatoes, fish pie or chicken dishes.

Curry sauce

2 onions

1 clove of garlic

2 oz/50 g butter or margarine

1 apple (1 large cooker or 2 small desert apples)

1 lemon

½ pint/150 ml of stock

1 tablespoon curry powder

2 tablespoons brown sugar

salt and pepper

Peel and chop the onions, garlic and apple. Squeeze the lemon. Melt the butter or margarine in a good sized frying pan and when hot add the chopped onions and garlic. Swet the onions in the fat, but do not let them burn or go brown. Stir in the curry powder. Add the apple and cook until tender, then add the lemon juice, stock, sugar, salt and pepper. Simmer for 20 minutes but do not boil. Take the sauce from the heat and allow to cool, then pour into a liquidiser or blender and whizz for 30 seconds. Re-heat before serving. This is a very versatile curry sauce and goes especially well with vegetable and chicken dishes. Serve with boiled or fried rice.

Barbara's Cream and White Wine Sauce – 1

This version of the sauce is best served with roast chicken (stuff the chicken with apple and lemon for excellent juice for the stock).

1 medium onion

chicken liver reserved from the bird to be cooked

2 tablespoons sunflower oil or 2 oz/50 g margarine

½ pint of vegetable stock – for example, water reserved from cooking carrots, potatoes, cabbage etc

juices from the cooked chicken

sugar, salt, pepper to taste

2 oz/50 g cream

½ glass of white wine

Fry the finely chopped onion in oil or margarine until golden brown. Add the finely chopped liver and fry until cooked through, stirring all the time. Add some of the juices from the cooking chicken and bring to the boil. Add ½ pint/150 ml of the vegetable stock, bring to the boil and then liquidise until smooth. Return the sauces to the pan and mix in the sugar and salt, then add the cream and ½ glass of white wine.

Barbara's Cream and White Wine Sauce – 2

This version of the sauce is for roast beef or pork dishes. Prior to cooking, marinate the meat overnight (or for as long as possible) in a mixture of mild mustard(⅔) and soy sauce(⅓), add finely chopped fresh root ginger to taste.

1 medium onion

1 pint of vegetable stock – for example, water reserved from cooking carrots,

leeks, broccoli etc

juices from the roast meat

sugar, salt, pepper to taste

2 oz/50 g cream

½ glass of white wine

1 tablespoon vinegar

Fry the finely chopped onion until golden brown. Add some of the juices form the roasted meat and ½ pint/150 ml of vegetable stock. Add a pinch of sugar, salt and the tablespoon of vinegar. Finally add the cream and wine.

Hot wine sauce

An excellent sauce to serve with grilled or barbecued fish.

1 lemon

4 tablespoons olive oil

1 large onion, chopped

4 fl oz/110 ml dry white wine

1 tablespoon salt

1 tablespoon freshly ground black pepper

2 oz/50 g chopped parsley

Peel and dice the lemon, taking care to remove all the pith and skin. Heat the oil and fry the onion. Add the prepared lemon and the wine and a seasoning of salt and pepper. Reduce the sauce over a high heat for about 5 minutes. Add the chopped parsley at the last moment. Serve immediately.

– Wales within your reach:
an attractive series
at attractive prices!

1. Welsh Talk
Heini Gruffudd
086243 447 5
£2.95

2. Welsh Dishes
Rhian Williams
086243 492 0
£2.95

3. Welsh Songs
Lefi Gruffudd (ed.)
086243 525 0
£3.95

4. Welsh Mountain Walks
Dafydd Andrews
086243 547 1
£3.95

The *It's Wales* series
is just one of a wide range
Welsh interest publications
from Y Lolfa.
For a full list of books currently in print,
send now for your free copy
of our new, full-colour Catalogue
– or simply surf into our website
at **www.ylolfa.com.**

*y***Lol***fa*

Talybont Ceredigion Cymru/*Wales* SY24 5AP
ffôn 0044 (0)1970 832 304 *ffacs* 832 782 *isdn* 832 813
e-bost ylolfa@ylolfa.com *y we* www.ylolfa.com